THE
BAHAMAS
RENAISSANCE

Locomotive Recol
No 45596 Bah

John Hillier

First published in 2019

British Library Cataloguing in Publication Data

A catalogue record for this book is available from the British Library.

ISBN 978 1 85794 509 6

Silver Link Publishing Ltd
The Trundle
Ringstead Road
Great Addington
Kettering
Northants NN14 4BW
Tel/Fax: 01536 330588
email: sales@nostalgiacollection.com
Website: www.nostalgiacollection.com

Printed and bound in the Czech Republic

Front cover: **AIS GILL** In a scene reminiscent of the glory days of steam No 45596 *Bahamas* is seen at the head of the 'Thames-Clyde Express' approaching Ais Gill on 31 August 1989. *John Cooper-Smith*

Title page: **TYSELEY** No 45596 *Bahamas* appears from behind classmate No 5593 *Kolhapur* during its 'launch' for Members, Donors and Supporters at Tyseley Locomotive Works on 28 September 2018. *JH*

Contents

About the author

John Hillier is the son of a career railwayman. His father started as a Premium Apprentice at the Great Eastern Works at Stratford before becoming a Technical Assistant to Sir Nigel Gresley. Subsequently he spent time in the railway workshops at Darlington, Stratford again, and latterly at Gorton where, as Works Manager, he had the unenviable task of closing the works in 1963. He then joined the HQ staff of BR Engineering.

It was therefore not unsurprising that John had an interest in railways and, living near Stockport, visited (bunked?) the shed at Edgeley regularly. It was on one of his many visits there in mid-1967 that he learned of the plans to save *Bahamas* and immediately became involved with the Bahamas Locomotive Society (BLS) as a 'Founder Member'.

Becoming responsible for publicity in the early days of the society, and after serving on the initial committee, he was appointed a Director of the company on its formation. Given his interest in photography – he was a member of the Railway Photographic Society from 1966 until its demise in 1976 and is still a member of the Rail Camera Club, its successor – it was natural that his camera should focus on No 45596 from time to time!

His work necessitated a move to Rutland from Cheshire, when his day-to-day involvement with the BLS ceased, but, when in 2010 he enquired about any plans to get *Bahamas* operational again and was then invited to take on the task of raising sufficient funds to achieve this, he became intimately involved once more. This resulted in him being asked to lead the project to submit a bid to what was then the Heritage Lottery Fund seeking financial help to overhaul the engine, and he subsequently led a small team to manage the project once a grant of £776,000 had been awarded.

Ever since he took on this challenge John has photographed all the key stages in the overhaul of the 'Jubilee', which was one of the commitments made to the National Lottery Heritage Fund. The large number of images he has amassed, together with his access to the BLS Archive and his contacts among fellow railway photographers, all proved to be excellent sources of material for this book.

The Golden Jubilee

The Society celebrated its 'Golden Jubilee' in June 2017 and met once again at the Crown Hotel in Stockport, the venue for its well attended weekly meetings 50 years before. It also announced – on 1 APRIL – that 45596 would be painted gold for a period so as to become a true 'GOLDEN JUBILEE'.

Interestingly *Bahamas* was outshopped in 1968 with paint supplied by Humbrol Ltd which generated comments about how many 14ml tins of model makers crimson lake paint had been used! Thus for our Golden Jubilee Humbrol were approached again and agreed to supply sufficient gold paint to transform *Bahamas*. It was estimated that 10 litres of paint would be needed, which meant that circa 715 small modellers pots would be required! Humbrol agreed to support our contribution to April Fools Day!

Thanks to John Cooper-Smith for showing what it would have looked like!

Acknowledgements

It was a pleasure to be asked by Peter Townsend from Silver Link Publishing to work on a book for SLP's 'Recollections' series about No 45596 *Bahamas*, which I believe is the first time that any book in this series has concentrated on a single locomotive. In fact, what started as a 64-page production has turned into 80 pages, such is the amount of material that I have had access to, and some of this might even be used in a further publication that will concentrate solely on the overhaul of a steam engine! Peter and Will Adams, Silver Link's Editor, deserve a great vote of thanks for their forbearance as unavoidable delays with No 45596's overhaul kept pushing back the publication date. There were other delays as we wanted to include No 45596's first public launch, its first trains and its subsequent 'commissioning' by Sir Peter Hendy, Network Rail's Chairman, in March 2019.

Many thanks are also due to the many friends and colleagues who have delved into their own photographic archives following my request for pictures; while I have used many of these excellent images, sadly it has not been possible to include all of them in this story about *Bahamas*. I hope that I have correctly recorded the authors of all the images used, but if not my sincere apologies.

I must also acknowledge help from the Mitchell Museum in Glasgow, where the North British records are held, the National Railway Museum and the Science Museum, where Ed Bartholomew helped identify suitable images, as well as Brian Stephenson's extensive archive, Martin Welch, and Graham Nicholas who, with Paul Shackcloth, was able to help with material from the Manchester Locomotive Society's extensive collection.

In addition thanks to Brian Dodson and colleagues for researching the SLS Collection of images. Thanks also to my colleagues in the Bahamas Locomotive Society for their support, since without their efforts *Bahamas* would not be running again; in particular I would like to thank my colleagues in the Project Team (Steve Allsop, Frank Galvin and David Guest, who took over from Mike Holmes), and the BLS Archivist Peter Skellon for his help. I must place on record that what has been achieved with *Bahamas* is very much down to the whole BLS team, as getting the engine working again has required the skills and dedication of everyone.

It goes without question that I must thank the National Lottery Heritage Fund and also the many thousands of people who have purchased Lottery tickets, as this made it possible for No 45596 to steam once more.

Bob and Alastair Meanley and all involved with No 45596's overhaul at Tyseley must also get a mention as they had to put up with your author turning up at odd times and at regular intervals to record yet another stage of their work; without their dedication and that of the workshop staff there, the locomotive would not be operating .

Unfortunately there will be some people whom I should also have thanked, so I apologise if I have not mentioned you individually. I do, however, feel that I should thank my family – and in particular Ann, my long-suffering wife – for their tolerance since *Bahamas* became part of my life once again. Much to my surprise and delight they all turned up unexpectedly when No 45596 was on view for the first time at Tyseley last September!

John Hillier
Barrowden
June 2019

LMSR No 45596 *Bahamas* is unique; it has a very interesting provenance, which this book attempts to describe and illustrate. The engine, which was built in Glasgow by the North British Locomotive Company in 1934, was the very last steam engine experimented on by British Railways in its attempt to improve the performance of its fleet of steam locos. This was the fitting of its double chimney and blastpipe at Crewe Works in May 1961 (see pages 13, 20 and 21). This fact was not known when a disparate group of steam enthusiasts formed the embryonic Stockport (Bahamas) Locomotive Society in July 1967 in an attempt to buy, preserve, overhaul and hopefully operate No 45596; their endeavours were successful and they managed to buy the locomotive from BR in September 1967.

Bahamas was the first locomotive of its class – the originally 191-strong 'Jubilee' Class of 4-6-0 engines designed by Sir William Stanier for the London Midland & Scottish Railway Company – to be saved, and its purchase resulted in the subsequent preservation of two further members of the class, both of which were then languishing in a scrap yard at Barry in South Wales. No 45690 *Leander* was saved from being cut up in 1972, whilst No 45699 *Galatea* emerged some time later in 1980. BLS Member Brian Oliver was responsible for initiating the preservation of both engines. A further member of the class, No 5593 *Kolhapur*, was saved and is currently part of the collection based at Tyseley Locomotive Works in Birmingham (see page 70).

No 45596 had been withdrawn from service in June 1966 after running hot on a rail tour from Carlisle (see page 18) and was placed in store at the rear of Stockport Edgeley Shed (9B) where it soon attracted interest from steam enthusiasts descending on the North West, all keen to witness the 'last rites' of BR's steam operations. After arriving from Carlisle Upperby Motive Power Depot (12B) in July 1962, *Bahamas* had become a local favourite engine, particular of 9B's Shedmaster Terry Smith, who expressed the hope that it might be saved. Classmate No 45632 *Tonga* had arrived at Edgeley with *Bahamas* primarily for hauling the overnight Aberystwyth to York train between Stockport and Leeds. After *Tonga* was transferred to Newton Heath in August 1965 – where it was withdrawn after a couple of months in October 1965 – No 45596 was used on a variety of lesser duties from 9B – and a number of special enthusiasts' trains – before it eventually ended up in the former Sand Sidings at Edgeley, where withdrawn engines were stored before disposal.

Thanks to what was probably the first attempt by a local community group to save a main-line steam loco, *Bahamas* was bought for £3,000 with the help of a loan from local businessman Geoffrey Potter in September 1967, and was immediately hauled to the Hunslet Engine Company in Leeds for repair (see page 23). It emerged in steam once more in March 1968 and returned to 9B resplendent in a quasi-LMSR crimson lake livery carrying the number 5596.

Bahamas was one of the few engines selected by BR to pioneer the 'Return to Steam' main-line trains in the early 1970s (see page 29) before it needed a further overhaul, this time undertaken by BLS volunteers themselves. The work was completed by 1988 – at a cost of just £15,000 – and the loco, by then in authentic BR green livery, hauled several rail tours before its main-line boiler certificate ran out in 1994. After use on a few heritage lines, it was eventually placed in store at Oxenhope on the Keighley & Worth Valley Railway (KWVR) in December 1997 (see page 48).

YORK No 45596 *Bahamas* and 'King' Class No 6000 *King George V* pose in the National Railway Museum in 2013. Both engines were involved with No 45596's first trip after preservation in October 1972 (see page 33). The juxtaposition of these two LMSR and GWR engines was appropriate given the influence that Swindon had on Stanier's designs when he became CME for the LMSR on 1 January 1932. *JH*

A campaign, 'Steams Last Blast', was initiated in 2011 to raise funds for a further overhaul and, after support from the National Lottery Heritage Fund and a project that cost about £1 million, *Bahamas* steamed for the first time for 21 years on 27 September 2018 at Tyseley Locomotive Works, from which it emerged behind Tyseley's own 'Jubilee' No 5593 *Kolhapur* (see page 70).

No 45596 *Bahamas* hauled its first trains in February 2019 with two 'sell-out' runs over the Settle & Carlisle line from its KWVR base.

No 45596 Bahamas shed allocations		
Shed	**Code**	**Allocated to**
Built		26 December 1934
Crewe North	5A	12 January 1935
Preston	10B (24K)	4 May 1935
Aston	3D (21D)	4 January 1936
Camden	1B	3 July 1937
Willesden	1A	28 August 1937
Crewe North	5A	4 December 1937
Camden	1B	18 December 1937
Crewe North	5A	1 January 1938
Camden	1B	16 April 1938
Crewe North	5A	30 April 1938
Camden	1B	2 July 1938
Kentish Town	14B	30 July 1938
Derby	17A	23 September 1939
Grimesthorpe	41B	2 March 1940
Millhouses	41C	6 September 1941
Bristol	22A (82E)	12 April 1947
Crewe North	5A	13 September 1947
Edge Hill	8A	28 August 1948
Carlisle Upperby	12B	24 February 1956
Stockport Edgeley	9B	21 July 1962
Withdrawn	9B	23 July 1966

STOCKPORT No 45596 is captured on shed at Stockport Edgeley (9B) in 1965 after the application of a yellow stripe (see page 63). *Les Nixon*

The 'Jubilee' Class

These 4-6-0 three-cylinder locos were designed by William Stanier, who was persuaded to leave the GWR at Swindon to become the LMSR's CME at Crewe.

His initial task was to evaluate the existing designs and to make recommendations to improve the performance of the LMSR fleet after its troubled years following the depression of the late 1920s.

His evaluation concluded that all of the LMSR's traffic could be worked by six standard designs, and a 4-6-0 with 6ft 9in driving wheels was one of them.

The 4-6-0 would have to contend with the various loading and weight restrictions on the LMSR system, and powerful enough to maintain strict timings.

By opting for a three-cylinder loco, Stanier was able to solve the quandary of having a powerful front end within the loading gauge, thus satisfying the civil engineer's constraints and the LMSR's operating requirements.

Two of the 'Jubilees', Nos 45735 *Comet* and 45736 *Phoenix*, were rebuilt with some different features, including a larger boiler and a double chimney, in 1942.

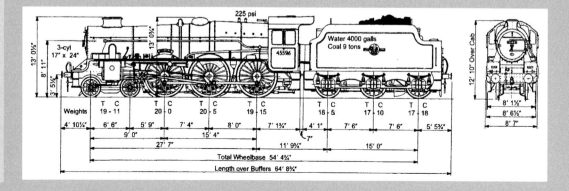

were seeking to break into markets previously dominated by British producers.

Although the new business had a capacity on paper of about 700 engines per annum, NBL never managed to attain that figure. Between the World Wars the company ran into difficulties thanks to fluctuating domestic demands, and work was therefore concentrated at the Hyde Park and Queen's Park premises.

After the Second World War there was a small revival, but NBL was unable to fully make the transition from steam to diesel and electric traction. Its last steam loco was built in 1958, and the business closed in 1962.

Of the four 'Jubilees' preserved, both *Kolhapur* and *Bahamas* were built at the Queen's Park Works in December 1934. *Leander* and *Galatea* were both built at Crewe in 1936.

Bahamas was built by the NBL as part of an order placed by the LMSR in 1933. NBL split the order in two, with 25 locos being built at each of its two works in Glasgow, Hyde Park and Queen's Park. *Bahamas* emerged from the latter on 26 December 1934.

The NBL tender for the 50 locos was £292,385 (£5,847 each), which was cheaper than the 10 built at the LMSR workshops at Derby (£6,039) and at Crewe (£7,244).

North British had been formed in 1903 as a result of the amalgamation of Sharp Stewart & Co, Neilson & Co and Dubs & Co, in an attempt to combat competition from manufacturers around the world that

GLASGOW Four 'Jubilee' locomotives are seen under construction at the NBL's Hyde Park Works. Twenty-five of these 4-6-0s were built there between 1934 and 1935. *Mitchell Library*

Above: **TEBAY** No 5596 speeds through Tebay Junction on 1 June 1935 with the 1.35pm Euston-Perth train. *H. C. Casserley, BLS Archive*

Left: **HEST BANK** This early view of No 5596, then unnamed, was taken at Hest Bank. It is allocated to 10B Preston, which suggests that this image was also taken in mid-1935. *BLS Archive*

Above: No 5596 apparently ex-works at Crewe is by now named *Bahamas* and fitted with a 'Fowler' high-sided tender with coal rails. *W. H. Whitworth, SLS Collection, MLS Archive*

Above right: No 5596 was named *Bahamas* in June 1936, when it also received the 3,500-gallon tender from 'Royal Scot' No 6129. *BLS Archive*

Right: **AIS GILL** *Bahamas* is captured by an unknown photographer approaching Ais Gill with a southbound express. The 4,000-gallon tender suggests that the picture was taken between May 1940 and October 1946. *BLS Archive*

Left: **OXENHOLME** Then unnamed and based at Preston (10B), No 5596 heads north at Oxenholme with a Liverpool to Glasgow down express in June or July 1935. The train conveys a GWR coach, which it is believed had started at Plymouth. The image has been coloured by Stephen Arrandale. *F. R. Hebron, Rail Archive Stephenson*

Left: **TRING** *Bahamas is seen at Tring in 1949 with an up express from Liverpool with 'Patriot' No 45507* Royal Tank Corps *in the siding. R. F. Dearden, National Railway Museum/Science & Society Picture Library*

Below left: **EDGE HILL** Seen at Liverpool Edge Hill (8A), at this time *Bahamas* is painted black and is coupled to 3,500-gallon tender No 9779, which was transferred from 'Patriot' No 5521 *Rhyl. H. C. Casserley, BLS Archive*

Below right: **CREWE** No 45596 is at Crewe North in 1952, painted green, at a time when it was shedded at Edge Hill. *Real Photos, National Railway Museum/Science & Society Picture Library*

Above left: **SHAP WELLS** On a wintry 22 February 1960 *Bahamas* is assisted at the rear near Shap Wells with a northbound freight. The fireman must feel that as the summit is close his work is over and that he has time to look out! *Derek Cross, David Cross*

Left: **TEBAY** *Bahamas*, hauling a southbound express, takes water on Dillicar troughs near Tebay on the West Coast Main Line (WCML) on 10 May 1956. *D. M. C. Hepburne-Scott, Rail Archive Stephenson*

Above: **WAVERTREE** No 45596 *Bahamas* departs with the 4.15pm down Birmingham train 29 July 1953. *Hewitt brothers, SLS Collection*

POWER CLASSIFICATION

The unrebuilt 'Jubilees' were given a 5XP power classification, which became 6P when the classification arrangements were modified in January 1951. It changed again in 1955 – when officially they became 6P5F – although the designation on the cabside remained '6P'.

No 45596's performance

Doug Landau, a renowned authority on steam performance, has this to say in an article describing No 45596's performance:

'I was fortunate to be on *Bahamas*' inaugural main-line rail tour, Derby-Didcot and return, on 27 May 1989. The departure from Derby seemed unusually swift and silent from my seat towards the end of the train. On arrival back at Derby the crowd gathered round *Bahamas were treated to an animated and colourful eulogy from the fireman:* "Whoever sorted out this engine did a ...... marvellous job." I don't know who first coined the epithet "Green Greyhound", but it was not long before this wonderfully apt description was attached to No 45596. The "Jubilees" certainly had the lean and racy lines of a thoroughbred racehorse or greyhound; the somewhat ungainly double chimney did, nevertheless, impart a certain regal air.

In March 1991 I received a log from David Veltom captioned: "Which loco do you think did this, with 440 tons? See inside small envelope for the answer!" The log revealed a fast climb northbound on the S&C; on the upper reaches of the climb, before an easing for signals intervened, the performance was approaching Class 8 "Pacific" territory; the unidentified contender in the envelope proved to be No 45596 *Bahamas*. Over the 3 miles from Helwith Bridge to milepost 244, before signal checks intervened, the level of performance was approaching maximum "Rebuilt Scot" prowess.

Better still was to come later that year in August 1991 working the "Welsh Marches" from Ludlow to Shrewsbury, with estimated equivalent drawbar horsepower as high as 1,800, very close to the best estimates for the "Rebuilt Scots" in BR days. The historic high water mark of "Jubilee" performance was set by No 5660 *Rooke* on dynamometer trials between Leeds and Bristol and return in October 1937. The maximum equivalent drawbar horsepower recorded was over 1,500, averaging 1,450 from Ormside to Ais Gill. *Bahamas*' peak efforts in August 1991 represented a 25% advance in drawbar performance. Based on such performances, the "Green Greyhound" could justly be dubbed a supercharged "Jubilee".

In its first preservation main-line incarnation No 45596 was operating under the 60mph limit. For its second innings the 75 limit will provide an opportunity to sport its "Green Greyhound" reputation; in particular new opportunities on Shap, Grayrigg and a host of other previously unavailable lines await.

As the ultimate example of belated steam improvement to appear in BR days, No 45596 is symbolic of missed opportunities generally on the part of British Railways, illustrating what, given a little more imagination, might have been.'

Liveries and tender types						
Date	Livery	Engine No	Tender Capacity	Tender No	From	Insignia
As built	LMS red	5596	4000	9043		LMS
8/6/36			3500 [1]	3925	Royal Scot 6129	
8/5/40			4000 [2]	9779	Patriot 5521	
11/10/46			3500 [1]	4485		
10/5/48	1946 LMS Black	45596	3500 [1]	4485		BRITISH RAILWAYS
24/7/52	BR green		3500 [1]	4485		Lion & wheel
18/6/54			3500 [1]	4248		
11/12/56			3500 [1]	3922		
Post 1958						Later crest
12/9/58			3500 [1]	4238		
17/1/59			3500 [1]	4492		
23/8/60			4000 [2][4]	9845		
5/10/63			4000 [2][3][5]	10750	48725/45717	Small crest
11/3/68	LMS red	5596	4000 [2][3][5]	10750		LMS
31/8/88	BR Green	45596	4000 [2][3][5]	10750		
27/9/18			4000 [2][3]	[10750]	New tank on original chassis	Large crest

[1] Fowler tender
[2] All welded
[3] Two spoked one disc wheel sets
[4] 9845 damaged at Farnley Junction. 9/63

[5] Tender 10750 was built for Class 8 48725 but transferred to 45717 *Dauntless* prior to being transferred to *Bahamas* on 5 October 1963 after the Farnley incident (see page16).

Far left: The Circular from LMR's Line Traffic Officer, Crewe, advising Motive Power Depots of the 'Experiment' on No 45596, undertaken with a view to improving its steaming.

Left: **CARLISLE** No 45596 waits for its next turn at Carlisle Upperby, to which it was transferred from Edge Hill in 1948. At the time it was fitted with a 3,500-gallon tender. *Gordon Coltas*

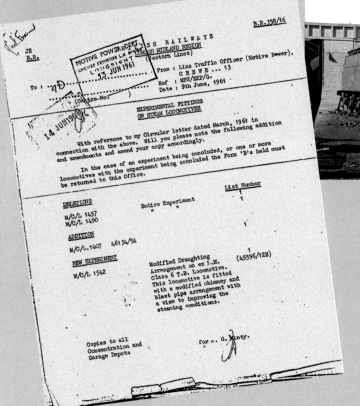

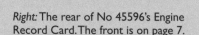

Right: The rear of No 45596's Engine Record Card. The front is on page 7.

Right **SHAP** Shortly after its double chimney had been fitted, *Bahamas* is seen making a storming ascent of the gradients at Shap on 1 July 1961. *Derek Cross, David Cross*

Bottom right: **SHAP** In the Summer of 1961 No 45596, with double chimney, hauls a freight near Shap Village. *T. G. Hepburn, Rail Archive Stephenson*

Below: **PENRITH** Carrying a 12B shedplate (Carlisle Upperby), *Bahamas* leaves Penrith with an up Keswick Convention Special on 21 July 1962. *Derek Cross, David Cross*

Above: **OXENHOLME** This shot of *Bahamas* bears interesting comparison with F. R. Hebron's picture on page 6, which shows the engine hauling 1S71, a Manchester to Glasgow express, at Oxenholme on 20 July 1963. *Colour Rail*

Above right: **SHAP** The same train is pictured at Shap Summit on 20 July 1963. *Rodney Lissenden*

Right: **EUXTON** No 45596 is seen heading along the WCML at Euxton Coal Sidings on 25 April 1962. *Peter Fitton*

Right: **FARNLEY JUNCTION**
Bahamas came into contact with a
Class 08 diesel shunter at Farnley
Junction, as a result of which its tender
became detached from its frame. The
ensemble is seen here at Farnley on 5
September 1963 ready for despatch
to Crewe. In the event it was taken to
Horwich Works. *Gavin Morrison*

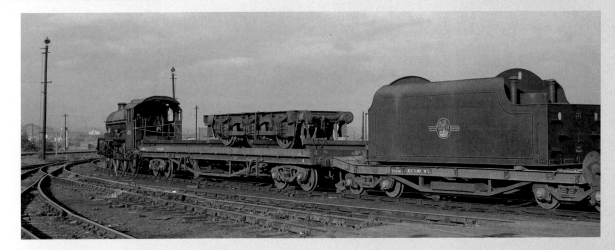

Right: **HORWICH WORKS**
13 October 1963 was the date of
the RCTS 'East Midlander No 6' rail
tour, which started from Nottingham.
Hauled for part of the trip by 'Crab'
No 42896, the tour visited both Crewe
and Horwich Works. At Horwich
participants were able to see *Bahamas*
and its damaged tender awaiting their
fate. Following a decision to withdraw
the loco, the powers that be eventually
relented to the pressure from Terry
Smith, the 9B Shedmaster, who wanted
his engine back! As a result *Bahamas*
was not withdrawn, and received a
replacement tender from 'Jubilee' No
45717 *Dauntless* (see page 12). *T. G.
Hepburn, Rail Archive Stephenson*

Above: **NEW MILLS** Despite being a 'favoured' engine at 9B, *Bahamas* was often rostered for local freight workings and is seen here in March 1963 during a stop at New Mills (Newtown) on the LNWR line to Buxton. *Bill Aveyard, MLS Archive*

Above: **LEEDS** At Copley Hill, Leeds, No 45596 *Bahamas* shunts some wagons on 22 April 1965, a less than prestigious but essential duty for the loco. The 'yellow stripe' advising that the engine was not allowed to run under the electric wires south of Crewe had been applied by this date. *Gavin Morrison*

Below left: **BUXTON** After being consigned to secondary duties towards the end of its BR career, *Bahamas* often appeared at Buxton on the 'Divi-shunt', the name by which the daily working from Edgeley was known, as it used to visit the Stockport Co-op Sidings en route. No 45596 is captured here on shed at Buxton, perhaps having worked this train, the 6.03am from Edgeley, on 12 May 1965. *J. M. Bentley*

Right: **YORK** *Bahamas* is seen under the coaling tower at York on 4 December 1965, where the train engines, Nos 45596 and No 45654 *Hood*, were serviced after an RCTS rail tour from Crewe. *Maurice Burns*

British Railways London Midland Region

Hunts Bank
Manchester 3.
Blackburn 3456   Ext. 2567   C. P. Midland   Divisional Manager

A. Bidder Esq.,
9 Denville Crescent,
Crossacres,
Wythenshawe,
MANCHESTER,22.

E101/147.

                                                      Date 27th April 1966.

Dear Sir,

                      Collectors Items.

        Thank you for your letter of the 20th instant, and I would
inform you the scrap metal price of old steam locomotives is at
present averaging from £34 to £40 a ton and the light weight of a
Class 5P Engine is approximately 73 tons.

        The minimum sale price therefore, would be in the region
of say £2,500 (quoted without prejudice) delivered to your local
station. This would no doubt involve you in additional expenditure
in transferring the locomotive to its proposed site, which may also
be subject to planning permission being given by the Local Authority.

        On receipt of your confirmatory letter of interest in this
matter I shall be pleased to refer your enquiry to the Chief Sales
and Contracts Officer of the British Railways Board.

                                Yours faithfully,

                                E. R. Kelly

                                for C.P.Millard.

British Railways Board

Evershot House
Evershot Street
London NW1   SUPPLIES MANAGER
Euston 3414   Ext. 160   Chief Supplies and Contracts Officer

G. Walker, Esq.,
18, Oldham Road,
MANCHESTER, 4.

y/r
o/r 17/230/522/227   October 31st, 1966.

Dear Sir,

                SALE OF LOCOMOTIVE NO. 45596

        Referring to our previous correspondence
and our discussion regarding the proposed sale of
the above mentioned locomotive.

        I have now ascertained from the Workshops
Authority that the cost of restoring this locomotive
to main line standards would cost £18,000.

        Our main Workshops are ceasing to repair
steam locomotives at the end of this year, and it
will be necessary for any instructions regarding
the repair of an outside locomotive to be in their
hands not later than the 8th November.

        Will you please let me know by return
what you wish me to do regarding both the sale and
restoration of this locomotive.

                                Yours faithfully,

                                for R.B. Hoff.

Right: **BLACKBURN** On 2 April 1965 *Bahamas* was one of four engines (*Flying Scotsman* and Nos 46426, 46458 and 45596) booked to haul the SLS/MLS 'Lakes & Fells' tour from Manchester to Penrith and Workington and back; this was the last steam passenger train to travel the length of the Penrith-Workington section. Although many trains in South Lancashire were cancelled as a result of a severe blizzard around Manchester, the train was given dispensation to run, although No 45596 had to wait for a snowplough to open the Blackburn to Hellifield section. No 4472 took over from *Bahamas* at Hellifield to run to Penrith via Carlisle, but the weather conditions played havoc with timings. No 45596 took over again at Hellifield for the return to Manchester, running very late. In this view *Bahamas* is seen at Blackburn – where it obviously came off the train briefly – before setting off for Hellifield in the snow. *Peter Fitton*

Right: **AIS GILL** The LCGB 'Fellsman' tour ran on 4 June 1966 from London Euston to Quintinshill and back using both steam and electric motive power. No 45596 *Bahamas* and classmate No 45593 *Kolhapur* were used on the Quintinshill to Crewe section via Ais Gill and Blackburn, and the two are seen here approaching the summit at Ais Gill. Unfortunately *Bahamas* ran hot on this section of the trip, which precipitated its withdrawal from service during the week ending 23 July 1966. It is thought that this was the last time that No 45596 ran prior to its preservation. *Brian Stephenson*

Top left: This letter dated 27 April 1966 from BR quotes a price of about £2,500 for the loco, which would be delivered 'to your local station'. It also pointed out that additional expenditure – and possibly planning permission – would be necessary in transferring it to 'its proposed site'.

Left: Following correspondence and discussions with the British Railways Board in London about 'LOCOMOTIVE No 45596', this letter from the Supplies Manager, British Railways Board, on 31 October 1966 quoted a price of

£18,000 to overhaul the engine to main-line condition. It stated that as the repair of steam locos was to cease at the end of 1966, it was necessary 'for any instructions regarding the repair of an outside locomotive' to be given within eight days! At that time the society had not been formed, there was no legal entity and no money!

Above: **STOCKPORT** *Bahamas* is captured easing gently on to the turntable at Stockport Edgeley on 26 March 1966, a day when it hauled the 'Eight Counties' rail tour for the RCTS. The train ran from Northampton, with No 45596 taking over from EM1 No 26000 *Tommy* at Godley Junction for the section to Crewe via Stockport (Tiviot Dale), Northwich and Middlewich. *Paul Ritchie*

Above right: **STOCKPORT** 9B's Shedmaster Terry Smith had given instructions that *Bahamas* should be specially cleaned for an Ian Allan Limited rail tour on 19 March 1966. The day before, the 18th, he is seen supervising the fitting of the engine's nameplate. Unfortunately the train was cancelled at short notice. It was thanks to Terry Smith that No 45596 was returned to service after 'the Farnley incident' and also for ensuring that the engine was stored away discreetly once it was taken out of service in July 1966 pending the hoped-for preservation of his favourite engine. *JH*

A

B

C

D

E

F

G

There has been much speculation as to whether the double chimney and blastpipe that make *Bahamas* unique – the other three remaining 'Jubilees' have single chimneys – were originally carried by No 45742 *Connaught*. This was the last member of the class to be built (in December 1936) and was fitted with a twin exhaust system in 1940, which it carried until it was removed in 1955 shortly before further twin-exhaust trials with the class took place at the Rugby test plant in 1957. Tests there with No 45722 *Defence* proved that modifications to the exhaust system increased both steam capacity and drawbar horsepower significantly, but the 1955 Modernisation Plan and the phasing out of steam traction terminated the planned further experimentation on the 'Jubilees'. However, BR's Circular M/C/L 1542 of June 1961 (see page 13) confirmed that a further experiment on *Bahamas* was undertaken when the loco had a 'Casual' repair at Crewe between March and May 1961 (see the Engine Card on page 13), using a design prepared at Derby in June 1960. This was the last experiment undertaken by BR to try to improve the performance of its steam fleet. Although there is no conclusive evidence either way, it is likely that No 45742's blastpipe was needed for No 45722's tests, then stored with the double chimney. Being in store with the drawings available, it was a cheap way of modifying No 45596. Although Shed Foremen were asked to report back to Crewe on the results from such experimental work, no such records have been found, although reports from loco crews and analyses of No 45596's performance do suggest it outperforms the single-chimneyed variants of the class.

The pictures on page 20 show:

A No 45742 *Connaught* at the head of 'The Midlander', a Wolverhampton-London Euston express. *Colour Rail*

B No 45596's old chimney (probably *Connaught*'s). *JH*

C The liners from No 45596's old chimney being removed. *Steve Allsop*

D The inside of No 45596's smokebox with the blastpipe in place. *BLS Archive*

E The blastpipe refurbished in 2018. *JH*

F The pattern for No 45596's latest double chimney. *Steve Allsop*

G A comparison between No 45596's chimney and the single chimney fitted to *Kolhapur*. *JH*

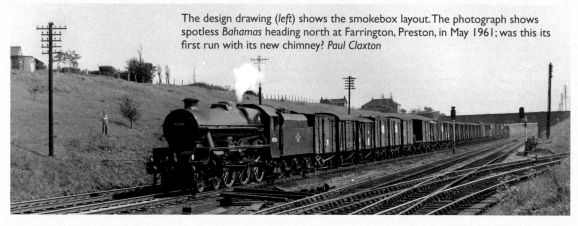

The design drawing (*left*) shows the smokebox layout. The photograph shows spotless *Bahamas* heading north at Farrington, Preston, in May 1961; was this its first run with its new chimney? *Paul Claxton*

FIGHT TO SAVE No 5596

MAY I appeal to all enthusiasts and public to help a group of friends and myself to retain the former LMS Railway Jubilee · class locomotive 5596 "Bahamas."

It is one of the last of its class still in existence, and it is our hope to have it eventually restored to the pre-war livery of maroon.

At present the locomotive is at Stockport Edgeley depot, where it has been stationed for the past six years, prior to withdrawal by British Railways.

It is our hope to keep her at the same depot. All depends on a successful outcome of discussions with British Railways, but I should be interested to hear from anyone who sympathises with the project.

A Bidder.
9 Denville Crescent,
Crossacres,
Manchester 22.

THIS

COULD BE REDUCED TO THIS

To prevent it the STOCKPORT (BAHAMAS) LOCOMOTIVE SOCIETY needs YOUR help.

This society has been formed for the purpose of acquiring and preserving "Bahamas" an ex – L.M.S.R. "Jubilee" class railway locomotive.

In many parts of the country steam traction has entirely disappeared and by the end of 1968 the run-down is expected to be complete. The only working examples of the steam locomotive, a symbol of an age of great achievement, will be those owned by private individuals or Societies like ourselves.

In order to place "Bahamas" in a main line running condition we are advised that the sum of £5,000 will be needed for a complete overhaul. The society then plans to run the locomotive as a monument to its designer, the late Sir William Stanier.

Far left: Alan Bidder's letter to the *Manchester Evening News* (27 April 1967), which sought support from readers.

Above: **STOCKPORT** No 45596 is seen in store in the Sand Siding at the rear of Stockport Edgeley MPD in about 1967. Alan Bidder's letter produced a response from Manchester businessman Geoffrey Potter, who agreed to loan £3,000 to the embryonic society. This generous offer enabled negotiations to take place with BR, and the eventual purchase in September 1967. A copy of the first appeal leaflet handed out widely to enthusiasts visiting the North West to witness the last rites of steam operations in the UK is also reproduced. JH

The Hunslet Engine Company

Right: **STOCKPORT** Type 2 No D5242 leaves Stockport hauling No 45596 *Bahamas* from 9B to Hunslet on 29 September 1967. *Martin Welch*

Below: **LEEDS** After arrival in Leeds, *Bahamas* is seen in the Erecting Shop at Hunslet Engine Company. *Hunslet Engine Company, BLS Archive*

Below right: **LEEDS** Work under way at Hunslet Engine Company on 14 October 1967. *JH*

Leeds was one of the earliest centres of locomotive building in the UK and several manufacturers based themselves in the Holbeck and Hunslet areas of the city. Locomotive building began in the early 19th century and continued for almost 200 years. Jack Lane, Hunslet, was a hive of activity with three famous builders – Manning Wardle & Company, Hudswell, Clarke & Company and the Hunslet Engine Company – all based there.

Hunslet was founded in 1864, its first loco appearing the following year. Over the years the company gained an enviable reputation for its shunting and industrial locos, which were sold worldwide.

The name 'Hunslet' became synonymous with the narrow-gauge 'Quarry' 0-4-0ST engines that were used in the North Wales slate quarries and of course the ubiquitous standard-gauge 'Austerity' 0-6-0STs, many of which were used in collieries until the 1980s; several are now preserved and used on heritage lines.

Jack Lane works closed in 1995, since when the business has processed through a succession of owners, some of which have designed and produced locos for specialised uses in a variety of settings.

A Civic Trust 'Blue Plaque' records that the company produced more than one-third of all the engines produced in Leeds.

LEEDS The Hunslet Engine Company's official photograph of *Bahamas*, 11 March 1968. *Hunslet Engine Company, BLS Archive*

Inset: During the time that No 5596 *Bahamas* ran in LMS livery, it carried the crest of the Bahamas Islands over its nameplate, acknowledging support from that country. Although many 'Jubilees' were named after British colonies and Commonwealth countries, only Nos 45595 *Southern Rhodesia* and 45739 *Ulster* carried geographical area crests during BR days. Also seen is the 1968 Hunslet worksplate and the 5596 numberplate. *JH, Keith Sanders*

LEEDS *Bahamas* is seen leaving the Hunslet Works in Jack Lane, Leeds, as it returns in steam to Stockport on 11 March 1968. In this fine study elements of 1960s industrial Leeds can still be seen. *Norman Harrop, MLS Archive*

BAHAMAS LOCOMOTIVE SOCIETY

Right: **STOCKPORT** *Bahamas*, having returned from Leeds, is displayed at 9B on 16 March 1968. Having run hot on the journey from Leeds on its return to Edgeley, the loco went to Longsight MPD on 22 March to use that depot's wheel drop. The defective axlebox was returned to Hunslet and refitted to *Bahamas* the next day. The engine then ran light from there to Buxton and back on 25 March; unfortunately no pictures of this unexpected trip, arranged at short notice, have been found. *Paul Ritchie*

Below: **STOCKPORT** Two rail tours had been arranged to run from Stockport to Carnforth and back on 17 March 1968 using Nos 4472 *Flying Scotsman* and 70013 *Oliver Cromwell*. At short notice the opportunity was taken to put them on display in the shed yard at Edgeley with No 5596 *Bahamas* on 16 March 1968. As both trains had sold out quickly and were oversubscribed, the BLS had hoped that its newly overhauled 'Jubilee' could haul a third train. Unfortunately permission was declined. *JH*

Right: **STOCKPORT** No 5596 glistens in the sun immediately after returning from Leeds on 11 March 1968, a spotless engine surrounded by grimy engines still in normal service. Shedmaster Terry Smith was elated! 'Britannia' No 70013 *Oliver Cromwell* is also seen. *JH*

Right: **BURY** As Edgeley was closing, BR kindly offered alternative accommodation at Bury steam shed, and *Bahamas* made the journey around Manchester to its new home on 26 March 1968. Permission was given for the loco to be steamed on 16 June, and it is seen here with Manchester-Sheffield Co-Co Class EM2 No 27005 *Minerva*, which was being stored there for a time. *BLS Archive*

DINTING No 5596 moved in steam from Bury to its new home at the ex-MS&LR steam depot at Dinting, Glossop, Derbyshire, on 15 November 1968, and by doing so broke BR's national ban on the use of steam locos anywhere on its network with the exception of *Flying Scotsman*. In this view *Bahamas* is seen crossing Dinting Viaduct prior to running on to the Glossop branch, which gave access to what became Dinting Railway Centre. *JH*

Above left: **DINTING** MPD was a sub-shed of Gorton (39A, subsequently 9G) and comprised a one-track through shed. The shed closed in 1935, although it reopened in 1942. In this fascinating pre-1955 view, Robinson 'C13' 4-4-2T No 67426 is seen adjacent to the coaling stage; it was one of a class kept at Dinting to run the Manchester to Glossop services. *John Hillier collection*

Above: **DINTING** Although Dinting closed to steam in 1954, it was used to stable electric engines as part of the Manchester-Sheffield-Wath 1500DC electrification programme. Here three Bo-Bo Class EM1s – including Nos 26022 and 26005 – are seen 'parked' adjacent to the shed building. *Neville Knight, John Hillier collection*

Above right: **DINTING** Following the arrival of *Bahamas*, the shed was branded 'Dinting Railway Centre' and became a popular attraction in North Derbyshire. This view was taken during the first Steam Weekend in April 1969. *JH*

THE 'BAHAMAS' LOCOMOTIVE SOCIETY

STEAM WEEKEND

APRIL 4th to APRIL 7th, 1969

AT THE

DINTING RAILWAY CENTRE

NEAR GLOSSOP - - DERBYSHIRE

Locomotives in Steam from 12 noon

ARPS Return to Steam Committee

STEAM LOCOMOTIVES APPROVED BY B.R.

Locomotive	Type	Depot
7029, Clun Castle	G.W. "Castle" 4–6–0	Tyseley
5593, Kolhapur	L.M.S. "Jubilee" 4–6–0	Tyseley
5428, Eric Treacy	L.M.S. class "5" 4–6–0	Tyseley
7752	G.W. 0–6–0 pannier-tank	Tyseley
7760	G.W. 0–6–0 pannier-tank	Tyseley
4871	L.M.S. class "5" 4–6–0	Carnforth
4932	L.M.S. class "5" 4–6–0	Carnforth
5231	L.M.S. class "5" 4–6–0	Carnforth
5407	L.M.S. class "5" 4–6–0	Carnforth
4079, Pendennis Castle	G.W. "Castle" 4–6–0	Didcot
6998, Burton Agnes Hall	G.W. "Modified Hall" 4–6–0	Didcot
6106	G.W. 2–6–2 tank	Didcot
6697	G.W. 0–6–2 tank	Didcot
1466	G.W. 0–4–2 tank	Didcot
5322	G.W. 2–6–0	Caerphilly
6000, King George V	G.W. "King" 4–6–0	Hereford
92203, Black Prince	B.R. class "9" 2–10–0	Eastleigh
75029, The Green Knight	B.R. class "4" 4–6–0	Eastleigh
35028, Clan Line	S.R. "Merchant Navy" 4–6–2	Ashford Co.
4498, Sir Nigel Gresley	L.N.E.R. class "A4" 4–6–2	Durham
60019, Bittern	L.N.E.R. class "A4" 4–6–2	Leeds
532, Blue Peter	L.N.E.R. class "A2" 4–6–2	Didcot
5596, Bahamas	L.M.S. "Jubilee" 4–6–0	Dinting

DINTING Following BR's introduction of a ban on the operation of steam locos, the Association of Railway Preservation Societies (ARPS) formed a 'Return to Steam Action Group' to prepare a case for the return of a limited number of steam engines on certain BR routes. Capt Peter Manisty was ARPS Chairman and was instrumental in securing the preservation of numerous steam locos that would otherwise have been cut up. BLS Chairman George Davies was a member of the Action Group and is seen here (*above right*) when it met at Dinting on 2 November 1969; left to right are Brian Hollingsworth, Peter Manisty, Roger Bell, David Shepherd, George Davies, Mike Crew and Keith Rymer. In the other view (*above left*) the Committee is seen during a meeting on the Bluebell Railway. *JH*

Left: The railway preservation movement was elated when, in April 1972, BR gave approval to the trial operation of a limited number of steam locos over carefully chosen routes. This was the result of the work of the ARPS in conjunction with Peter Prior, MD of Bulmers Limited, that company having had custody of GWR 'King' No 6000 *King George V*, which it restored to running order. 'KGV' had hauled an initial train in October 1971, followed in 1972 by a few more trains. *Bahamas* was one of the engines selected to run again, and is now one of only a few engines on the 1972 list still able to run.

No 45596 Breaks the 'Steam Ban'

DINTING On 18 April 1971 approval was given by BR's Manchester Division for *Bahamas* to leave Dinting in steam and to travel along the 1-mile branch to the terminus at Glossop, thus breaking BR's ban on steam once again! No 45596 turned on the triangle at Dinting and did all of the work on the return journey, although Type 2 No 5155 was attached for 'safety reasons'! In the first picture (*top left*), taken by Martin Welch, excited BLS members mingle with BR Inspectors and staff on the coaling stage before the engine sets off (*top right*). It is then seen accessing BR metals for the first time and returning along the branch with the mill chimneys of this Derbyshire town still much in evidence. *JH (2)*

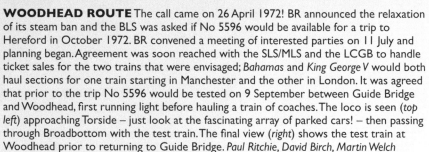

WOODHEAD ROUTE The call came on 26 April 1972! BR announced the relaxation of its steam ban and the BLS was asked if No 5596 would be available for a trip to Hereford in October 1972. BR convened a meeting of interested parties on 11 July and planning began. Agreement was soon reached with the SLS/MLS and the LCGB to handle ticket sales for the two trains that were envisaged; *Bahamas* and *King George V* would both haul sections for one train starting in Manchester and the other in London. It was agreed that prior to the trip No 5596 would be tested on 9 September between Guide Bridge and Woodhead, first running light before hauling a train of coaches. The loco is seen (*top left*) approaching Torside – just look at the fascinating array of parked cars! – then passing through Broadbottom with the test train. The final view (*right*) shows the test train at Woodhead prior to returning to Guide Bridge. *Paul Ritchie, David Birch, Martin Welch*

ALTRINCHAM and SHREWSBURY As no problems were experienced on the trial runs with No 5596, final preparations were made for its first run. These included making arrangements to run *Bahamas* light from Dinting to its stabling point at Hookagate, just outside Shrewsbury, on 12 October 1972. The engine is seen here (*left*) running towards Skelton Junction near Timperley, and again (*top*) on arrival being prepared on 13 October in readiness for its rail tour the following day. *JH*

Opposite: **LUDLOW** *'Bahamas, wishing you every success on Saturday. Black Prince and Green Knight'* ran the text of a telegram received from David Shepherd and his engines on 14 October in Stockport. Meanwhile in Shrewsbury a resplendent 'Jubilee' was waiting for the ex-Manchester section of the train to arrive. At the time the maximum allowed speed was 60mph; the train arrived at Hereford slightly early and No 5596 eventually moved off to the Bulmer Railway Centre for servicing (see page 34).

Welsh Marches Rail Tour

Saturday 14th Oct. 1972

Presented with the compliments of Williams & Glyn's Bank

These images show the southbound train leaving Ludlow Tunnel (*right*) with the ex-Manchester SLS/MLS train and again when pausing at Ludlow with the ex-London LCGB train while heading north to Shrewsbury later in the day. At Shrewsbury No 5596 hooked off and arrived back at Dinting at about 21.00hrs. At Ludlow, the driver, attired in the BR headgear of the time, appears very satisfied with the engine's performance. *John Whiteley (right), Don Benn (above and top)*

HEREFORD At Bulmers Railway Centre (*top left*) *Bahamas* was checked and serviced for its return to Shrewsbury with the LCGB train from London that *King George V* had hauled from Newport. In the other two shots the crowds gather round both engines as they change over, No 6000 having arrived from the south. Fortunately fewer people are on the track to watch *Bahamas* depart with the final steam-hauled section of the journey. *Bahamas* performed perfectly throughout the day. *Paul Richie, Norman Kneale (2)*

CHINLEY and SHEFFIELD 17 June 1973 saw a 'Jubilee' in LMS livery work once again over part of the Midland Main Line when *Bahamas* hauled trains between Guide Bridge and Sheffield in both directions. This time the BLS managed the ticketing of the two proposed trains, once again with one starting in Manchester and the other in London. Unfortunately the train from London failed to attract sufficient bookings and was cancelled. As a result *Bahamas* was stabled at Grindleford while waiting for the train to return from Scarborough. This was the first steam-hauled train to traverse the Edale Valley since 1968, and it is seen (*left*) at Chinley East Junction and at Millhouses (*right*) on the return leg. *John Whiteley, Peter Fitton*

THE BAHAMAS LOCOMOTIVE SOCIETY
INVITES YOU TO TRAVEL BEHIND STEAM THROUGH THE
BEAUTIFUL PEAK DISTRICT AGAIN ON
SUNDAY, JUNE 17th, 1973

"THE SCARBOROUGH LIMITED"

Manchester Piccadilly (approx. 08.15), Guide Bridge (pu), Sheffield, York, Scarborough and return.
Motive power includes:
LMSR 4-6-0 No. 5596 "BAHAMAS" (Guide Bridge/Sheffield/Guide Bridge)
LNER 4-6-2 No. 19 "BITTERN" (York/Scarborough/York)
Refreshment facilities
£5·75 (children, limited, £4·75)
Details/bookings: G. C. Davies, c/o Williams & Glyn's Bank Ltd., 572 Stockport Road, Longsight, Manchester M12 4JJ

"THE DERBYSHIRE BELLE"

London St. Pancras (approx. 08.15), St. Albans (pu), Luton (pu), Bedford (pu), Sheffield, Guide Bridge, Dinting (for visit to Railway Centre) and return.
Motive power includes:
LMSR 4-6-0 No. 5596 "BAHAMAS" (Sheffield/Guide Bridge/Sheffield)
Refreshment facilities
£4·95 (children, limited, £3·95)
Details/bookings: K. J. Tait, 15 Priestnall Road, Heaton Mersey, Stockport, Cheshire

**A foolscap S.A.E. must be enclosed with each booking or enquiry
An additional S.A.E. should be sent if an acknowledgement of booking is required**

DINTING and REDDISH On 8 September 1973 *Bahamas* was invited to attend an Open Day at Reddish Electric Depot (*right*), and is seen (*below*) crossing Dinting Viaduct hauling 'J94' 0-6-0ST No 44/7136 – which was in the Erecting Shop at Hunslet when No 5596 was under repair there – and SR 'Schools' 4-4-0 No 30925 *Cheltenham*, together with the BLS coach and brake van. There is a remarkable lack of traffic on the A57. Just as it had done at Bury in 1968, the 'Jubilee' was asked to shunt some of the electrics on view that day.

This was the last working of *Bahamas* during its first period of running in private ownership, its boiler certificate expiring. However, Brian Oliver, a BLS member, had been so impressed with No 45596 that he decided to extract No 45690 *Leander* from the scrap lines at Barry Island, South Wales, and have it restored in authentic LMS livery; thus all the energies of the society were then devoted to running No 5690, which had been extensively overhauled by BR Derby. *Leander* arrived at Dinting on 25

August 1973 and hauled its first train on 1 September. Unfortunately the two red 'Jubilees' were never in steam together at Dinting. *Martin Welch*

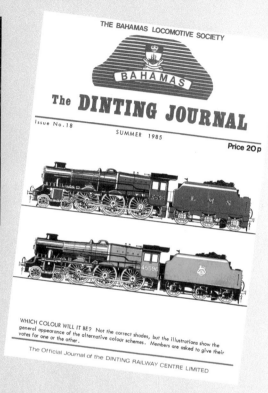

THE BAHAMAS LOCOMOTIVE SOCIETY

BAHAMAS

The **DINTING JOURNAL**

Issue No. 18

SUMMER 1985

Price 20p

WHICH COLOUR WILL IT BE? Not the correct shades, but the illustrations show the general appearance of the alternative colour schemes. Members are asked to give their votes for one or the other.

The Official Journal of the DINTING RAILWAY CENTRE LIMITED

DINTING BLS volunteers began overhauling *Bahamas* at Dinting and, at a cost of just £15,000, this was completed in time for the society's 21st birthday celebrations in 1988. These pictures show the engine at various stages of its overhaul at Dinting – the boiler lift in September 1981 (*top left*) and green paint being applied on 31 July 1988 (*bottom left*) in readiness for the birthday event on 25 September (*top middle*). Members were asked in 1985 to vote for the colour in which No 45596 should be painted when the overhaul was complete. The result? Green 192. Red 173. *Steve Allsop, Martin Welch, JH*

LOADED TEST RUN Following the overhaul No 45596 moved to Butterley in readiness for its loaded test train around the Derby/Sheffield circuit on 18 May 1989, seen here leaving Sheffield (*left*) followed by a Derby/Didcot/Derby special on 27 May 1989, seen at Hatton (*top right*) and leaving Derby (*bottom right*). The engine was also used on a series of shuttles between Nottingham (*bottom left*) and Derby on 4 June 1989. JH, Malcolm Ranieri, John Cooper-Smith (2)

BORROWASH, LOSTOCK AND BOLTON A further view of the Nottingham - Derby shuttles on the left at Borrowash in June 1989. Two of the Manchester - Southport shuttles are seen at Lostock (top right) and Bolton (bottom) on 17 September 1989 *Malcolm Ranieri, Peter Fitton, John Crawshaw*

STOKESAY CASTLE and MARSHBROOK *Bahamas* put in some outstanding performances on the Welsh Marches route, particularly on 3 August 1991 where it surpassed all previous peak

drawbar performances for a 'Jubilee' at that time on the rising grades towards Church Stretton heading north. In these views, both taken on 26 March 1994, No 45596 is seen powering south near Stokesay Castle (*left*) and a little earlier further north at Marshbrook (*above*). *Malcolm Ranieri, JH*

To Holyhead

PENMAENBACH, BANGOR and CHESTER The 'Jubilee' also made several forays along the North Wales coast between Crewe and Holyhead, and is seen here heading west at Penmaenbach (*left*), leaving Chester (*bottom right*) on 15 September 1991, and at Bangor (*right*) on 27 May 1991. *All JH*

SETTLE & CARLISLE Although the 'Jubilees' were able to work virtually anywhere in their declining years, it was their performances over the Settle & Carlisle line that attracted most attention. It was perhaps understandable that it was to the S&C that enthusiasts tended to flock to see *Bahamas* at work or to travel behind it. In these views *Bahamas* is seen southbound at Baron Wood near Armathwaite (*above left*) on 31 August 1989, southbound again at Angrholme just north of Ais Gill on 13 April 1991, and northbound having just left Blea Moor Tunnel on 29 June 1902. *Peter Zabek, Brian Dobbs, Keith Sanders*

SETTLE & CARLISLE

Some further views of No 45596 at work over the S&C route. It is seen leaving Skipton on 4 October 1992 (*top left*) heading north, approaching Ais Gill with the southbound 'Royal Scotsman' train (*top right*) on 30 April 1991, and pulling away from Settle Junction heading north with a Keighley Business Forum train to Carlisle on 19 October 1991 (*bottom*). *Maurice Burns, John Cooper-Smith, John Crawshaw*

BIRKETT TUNNEL On 11 August 1993, the 25th anniversary of BR's last steam train, *Bahamas* and No 44871, the latter having been used on the final train on 11 August 1968, climb south towards Ais Gill. It was a privilege for the Bahamas Locomotive Society to be asked to help with the motive power for this anniversary train. *Maurice Burns*

SCARBOROUGH, GCR, GWSR and ELR No 45596
Bahamas retired from main-line duties on 18 September 1994 after
hauling a Bradford/Scarborough/Bradford train, its main-line boiler
certificate having expired. The train is seen (*top left*) passing under
the renowned signal gantry at Falsgrave near Scarborough. The engine
then visited a number of heritage railways before its boiler certificate
finally expired in December 1997, and it is seen here on the East
Lancashire Railway exiting Nuttall Tunnel in the autumn of 1993 (*top
right*), on the Great Central Railway on 1 July 1995 double-heading
with *Kolhapur* (*bottom left*), the Nene Valley Railway in 1995, where
the Duke of Kent visited the footplate on 6 June 1995 (*centre*), and
on the Gloucestershire Warwickshire Steam Railway on 30 August
1997. *Adrian Scales, John Crawshaw, Simon Bryant, Malcolm Ranieri, JH*

ELR, PADIAM, SVR and LONGSIGHT No 45407, *Bahamas* and *Black Prince* are seen at Buckley Wells, on the East Lancashire Railway, on 15 October 1994 (*top left*), quite a nostalgic reunion given No 45596's previous visit to the shed (see page 27) and the telegram received from No 92203 (see page 32). Also seen is the 4-6-0 at Padiam Power Station Open Day (7 October 1989), its visit to the Severn Valley Railway (April 1994) and (*below*) Longsight MPD in 25 April 1992. *Mike Heath, John Crawshaw, David C. Williams, Mike Heath*

OXENHOPE and HAWORTH In 1990 the BLS moved its headquarters from Dinting to Ingrow on the Keighley & Worth Valley Railway (KWVR), which had offered the society use of the Ingrow goods shed as the BLS could no longer afford the increased rent at Dinting. The KWVR offered access to the S&C as well as an opportunity to run on this idyllic 5-mile branch line. These shots show *Bahamas* at work on its new 'home' railway: approaching Oxenhope (*top left*) on 18 August 1990, approaching Haworth (*top right*) on 31 March 1990, and at rest at Haworth shed alongside the other BLS locos, *Nunlow* and the LNWR Coal Tank No 1054, on 29 October 1991. *Mike Heath, John Cooper-Smith, Mike Heath*

From: John Hillier

Sent: Monday, June 21, 2010 12:54 AM

To: Simon Bryant

Subject: AGM

Hi Simon,

During the AGM and since I have been giving some thought to Bahamas and the need to raise further funds and hopefully the following might be useful in the debate as to how to proceed. Please accept these as my musings; they imply no criticism at all to the excellent work done so far by 'the few' but are my own thoughts as possible courses of action....and of course I accept that you will probably have already had detailed discussions as to how you might proceed.

Main Line or not?

BAHAMAS MEETING, LOUGHBOROUGH, WEDNESDAY 4 AUGUST 2010

Notes compiled at the meeting (not a complete record by any means).

Yes to restoration of loco to main line operating condition.

Could take three years to do up.

A decision on whether the locomotive needs to be fitted with air brakes for operational or commercial reasons need not be taken until six months before completion of the work.

EDGELEY and OXENHOPE

In June 2010, following the BLS AGM, the author decided to initiate an enquiry (*far left*) to see if *Bahamas*, resident inside Oxenhope shed (*below right*) since December 1997 could be overhauled as a tribute to those friends from the early days of the society who had sadly passed away. Subsequently a brainstorming session was held at Loughborough on 4 August 2010, at which the provenance of No 45596 was discussed in detail for the first time. The important role that *Bahamas* had played in the development of steam performance had not been appreciated when the engine was bought 43 years earlier – the double chimney and blastpipe became No 45596's Unique Selling Point! The picture on the far left shows the engine under repair at Edgeley in September 1965 with the blastpipe clearly visible on the running plate. *Peter Fitton, Peter Skellon*

YORK The BLS members had been raising funds for many years and following review of possible options, the Society agreed to launch the 'Steam's Last Blast Appeal' and also agreed to submit a bid to the Heritage Lottery Fund for help. The bid documents were lodged with the HLF – now the National Lottery Heritage Fund – on 31 May 2012, which coincided with the beginning of the Railfest event at York's National Railway Museu (see right), to which both the LNWR Coal Tank and *Bahamas* had been invited. This was No 45596's first move away from the KWVR since 1997. For several months after the end of Railfest, *Bahamas* was displayed in the Great Hall of the Museum (above). *JH*

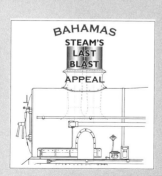

BAHAMAS
STEAM'S
LAST
BLAST
APPEAL

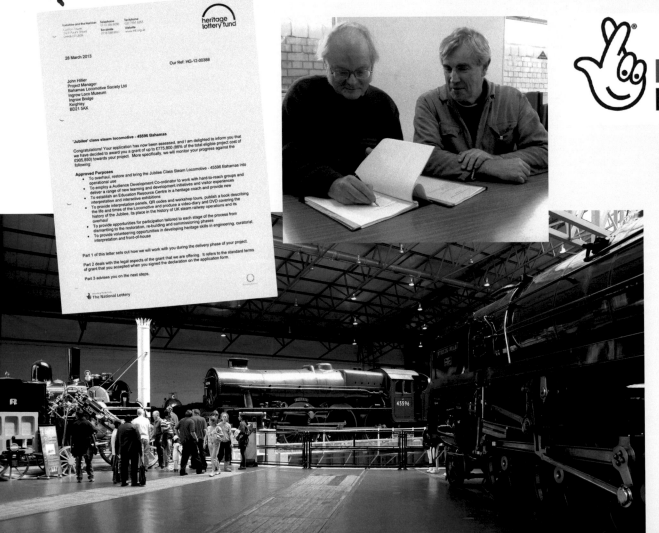

YORK and TYSELEY

This picture (*bottom*) captures the provenance of *Bahamas* alongside *Rocket* – replica! – and No 92220 *Evening Star* – all 'firsts' or 'lasts'! The BLS heard from the HLF on 28 March 2013 that its bid had been accepted and, having kept its intentions fairly confidential, surprised many in the heritage movement with the news of a £776,000 grant. The total project was estimated at £906,000, which included a major educational initiative in addition to the overhaul of *Bahamas*, the biggest it had had since 1959. Tyseley Locomotive Works tendered successfully for the work and its then Managing Director, Bob Meanley, is seen signing the contract with Steve Allsop, the BLS Chief Engineer, on 31 October 2013. *JH*

INGROW, HORNCASTLE and TYSELEY The contract having been signed, No 45596 left Ingrow on 26 November 2013 and travelled to Tyseley via the offices of Mortons Media, publishers of *The Railway Magazine* and *Heritage Railway* for display the next day. Many schools and townsfolk came to see the loco and the visit was featured extensively on local radio, TV and the press. *Bahamas* arrived at Tyseley in the early hours of 28 November and is seen here waiting to be offloaded. *JH*

This diagram illustrates the extensive repairs needed to the boiler. While much of the work was expected and planned for (marked in green), the red areas show how much additional work was needed. The decision to increase the extent of the repair was made in the hope that the boiler would be 'fit for purpose' for as long as possible and not just for the expected life of the boiler tubes. *Drawing by Steve Allsop*

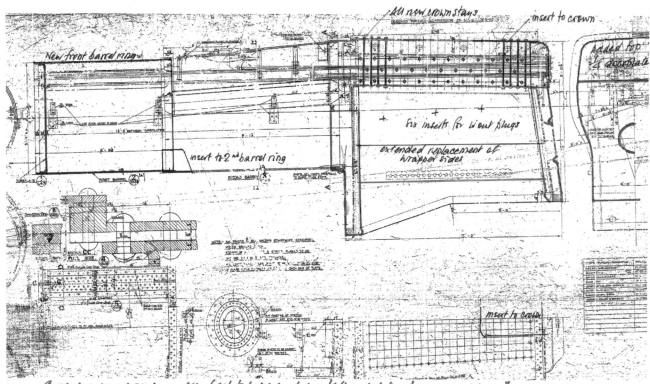

Green: original scope — New front tubeplate, bottom ½ throatplate, ¼ wrappersides, ¾ doorplate

Red: extra's — front barrel ring, inserts in second barrel ring & crown, wrapper sides increased to ⅓, doorplate increased to complete, 6 inserts in upper wrapper for w'out plugs. All crown stays

TYSELEY Although No 45596 had arrived at Tyseley in November 2013, work on its repair did not commence properly until January 2014. An iconic moment in the engine's overhaul took place on 16 January 2014 when its boiler was removed from the frames using Tyseley's steam crane (*left*). Earlier that morning the locomotive, minus cab, could be seen (*top right*) in Tyseley's new workshop alongside the frames of the new-build 'Patriot' 4-6-0 No 5551/45551 *The Unknown Warrior*. The other shot (*bottom right*) shows the inside of the frames without the boiler, a view rarely seen. *JH*

TYSELEY These four shots show some progress with No 45596's repair during the early months of 2014. Steve Allsop, BLS's CME, is seen assessing progress with the boiler (*top left*). Next we see work under way to repair cracks that had been found around the horn gaps (*top right*), the driving wheel sets removed, and the chassis standing in the workshop; the tender from GWR No 7029 *Clun Castle* can also be seen. What cannot be shown is all the associated administrative work needed with the insurance company and discussions as to how to repair the whole boiler to the required standard. A lot of other work on the tender and pipework was also under way at Ingrow. *JH (3), Steve Allsop*

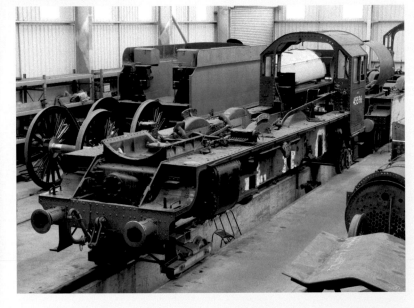

Hill & Webster Ltd, 2015

ASHBOURNE Seen here in January 2015 is the new tender tank – the old one leaked badly and was life-expired – showing the modifications to the lockers to accommodate the new electrical equipment needed to operate the engine safely on the modern railway. As space was at a premium, the water scoop was removed to provide additional room. The old tank had been modified to provide additional water capacity, which had reduced the amount of coal that could be carried; the coal space has been maximised in the new tender tank. *Steve Allsop*

BUCKFASTLEIGH These images were taken in June 2014 at South Devon Railway Engineering's workshops, where *Bahamas'* wheelsets had been taken to have new tyres fitted. The new tyres were manufactured in South Africa and the pictures show the wheel sets being prepared to receive them, then being lowered into place to accept the heated and expanded tyres. There is also a shot of the tyres being fixed to the wheels using Gibson rings, which are being pressed into place. *JH*

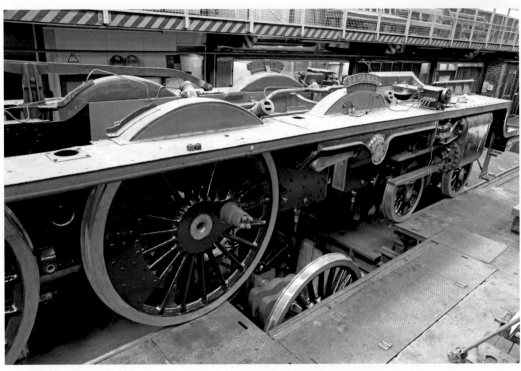

TYSELEY The wheel sets having been returned to Tyseley, the tyres are seen here being profiled on the wheel lathe in January 2015 before the wheels are returned to the frames using the wheel drop that is situated in the 'old' area of the Tyseley Workshops. *JH*

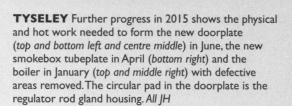

TYSELEY Further progress in 2015 shows the physical and hot work needed to form the new doorplate (*top and bottom left and centre middle*) in June, the new smokebox tubeplate in April (*bottom right*) and the boiler in January (*top and middle right*) with defective areas removed. The circular pad in the doorplate is the regulator rod gland housing. *All JH*

TYSELEY Here new crown stays are seen being fitted (*bottom right*), as is the new boiler platework, which required a certificated welding technique. These pictures were taken in April and June 2016. Meanwhile at Ingrow work proceeded on the overhaul of the lubrication system and injectors, as well as considerable work on overhauling the tender chassis. *All JH*

INGROW These images show some of the tasks under way at Ingrow, where BLS volunteers worked on most of the motion, cladding and a multiplicity of boiler and other parts. One large job was the fitting of the new tender tank to the refurbished chassis, a job that took place in November 2016 and used the BLS steam crane RS1015/50. *JH (2), BLS Archive (2)*

Left: **TYSELEY** Mid-2017 saw the new boiler tubes being cut to size and fed into the boiler, which by then had its new tubeplate fitted. *JH*

TYSELEY The powerhouse of *Bahamas* is the boiler, and these images show the first set of tubes being fitted. The superheater flues were X-rayed during May 2017, while at Ingrow all the mechanical refurbishment on the tender (hoses, brakes, water feed fittings, etc) was completed ready for its move to Tyseley to join the locomotive. *JH*

TYSELEY Towards the end of 2017 the foundation ring had been fitted and caulked and the boiler was ready for its hydraulic test, which was followed by an out-of-frames steam test. On 12 December your author had the privilege of lighting a fire in the boiler, its first for 20 years (*bottom left*). This was a warming fire before the successful steam test that took place on 21 December (*bottom right*). Ben Mason (bottom left), JH

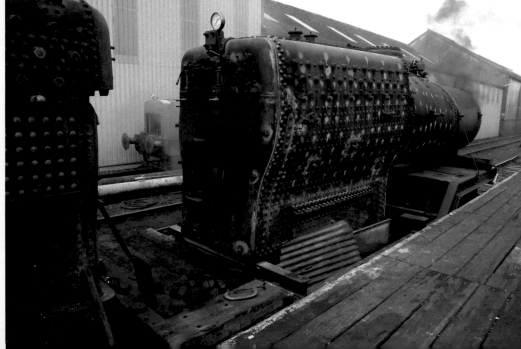

TYSELEY The 'official' steam test took place in the presence of the Boiler Inspector on 21 December 2017. He is seen watching the pressure rise (*top left*), and looking into the boiler with Alastair Meanley and Steve Allsop before finally signing off the test (*bottom right*). JH

Throughout the latter stages of the overhaul skilled society volunteers visited Tyseley regularly in order to undertake specific engineering tasks. In addition to CME, Steve Allsop, Steve Peach, Mike Stevens and numerous others spent many hours working on the locomotive.

The Yellow Stripe

From 1 September 1964, when additional sections of the West Coast Main Line were electrified, certain steam locomotives were prohibited from working 'under the wires' south of Crewe. An instruction was issued by the Drawing Office at Derby Works stating that 'Locomotives were to have a diagonal line painted six inches wide on the cab sides, the lowest point being adjacent to the cab footsteps. Lines to be painted yellow.'

The restriction applied to the 'Jubilees' and about 70 of the class remaining had the stripe painted on. It is reported that Passed Cleaner John Nixon, one of the ex-9B employees who attended the steaming of No 45596 on 27 September 2018 (see page 70), suggested that the stripe should be kept within the existing cabside lining rather than extend across the whole of the cab. This was agreed and *Bahamas* was one of only six 'Jubilees' painted this way. *Paul Ritchie*

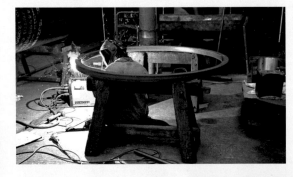

TYSELEY In 2018 the new smokebox is seen adjacent to the boiler, which has been fitted with some crinolines ready for the cladding to be fixed (in March) as work on the smokebox continues (April) and the new ashpan (*top right*) is fitted in June (*lower right*). *All JH*

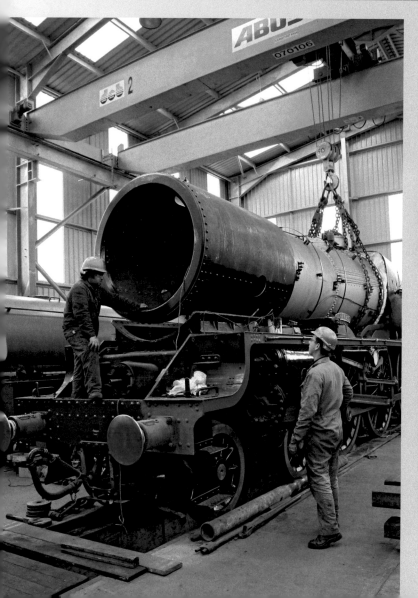

TYSELEY The picture of the refurbished frames (*near left*) bears interesting comparison with that on page 53. The other views show the boiler with the ashpan fitted being lowered gently into the frames (*far left*), and a rare view of the underside of the engine (*below*) in June 2018. *All JH*

TYSELEY The picture (*top left*) shows an almost visually complete *Bahamas* in August 2018. The main steam pipe, chimney, smokebox door and refurbished blastpipe are all awaiting fitting. The other images show the inside of the new smokebox and the new chimney being lowered into place.
All JH

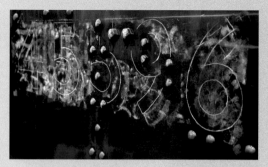

TYSELEY This series of pictures, taken in August 2018, shows the engine being prepared for painting, then the numbers, tender crest and green paint being applied. *All JH*

AUTOMATIC WARNING SYSTEM INDICATOR

STEAM CHEST PRESSURE GAUGE

INJECTOR STEAM VALVES

WHISTLE HANDLE

BOILER PRESSURE GAUGE

BRAKE VACUUM GAUGE

BRAKE EJECTOR STEAM VALVES

BOILER WATER LEVEL GAUGES

CARRIAGE WARMING PRESSURE GAUGE

SANDING VALVE

BLOWER VALVE

CONTINUOUS BLOWDOWN VALVE

SPEED INDICATOR

REGULATOR HANDLE

BRAKE VALVE

REVERSER

FIREHOLE

ASHPAN DAMPER-DOOR CONTROLS

THE FOOTPLATE The picture of No 45596's footplate (*above*) identifies the key footplate controls (with thanks to Peter Skellon for the annotation). On 1 July 1995 (*top left*) *Bahamas* was at work on the Great Central Railway – note the inscription above the driver's head. While the footplate will become more 'used' as time goes on, every attempt will be made to keep it in as spotless condition as is possible despite the rigours of operational use! *All JH*

TYSELEY No 45596 *Bahamas* moved under its own steam for the very first time for 21 years on 27 September 2018 when, with the sun beating down, it made several forays up and down the running lines within the confines of Tyseley Locomotive Works. It moved under the watchful eyes of Phil Bates, Nicky Morrant, Dean Morris and Alastair Meanley, just a few of the Tyseley team involved with the engine's 5-year major overhaul. *JH*

TYSELEY The engine was 'unveiled' to members, donors and an invited group of guests at Tyseley on Friday 28 September 2018, when BLS Patron, Lady Judy McAlpine, unveiled the nameplate by removing the Bahamas Islands and Union flags, assisted by BLS Chairman Keith Whitmore. The event was also attended by a group of former Edgeley staff (*near right*); left to right they are John Nixon (72), Edwin Bowlas (86), Eddie Rowbotham (91) and Alan Budge (71). *Bahamas* had been hidden away before emerging behind Tyseley's 'Jubilee', *Kolhapur. All JH*

TYSELEY The locomotive, in pristine condition, was on public view for the first time during Tyseley's Open Weekend on 29-30 September 2018. It was reported that *Bahamas* stole the show despite being surrounded by copper-capped engines at a well-known GWR location! *All JH*

TYSELEY Some more pictures of No 45596 during the Open Day. My publisher asked, 'Is that the infamous bucket of steam many young apprentices have been sent in search of?' *All JH*

Testing

TYSELEY, SMALL HEATH and STRATFORD-UPON-AVON

The testing of No 45596 was delayed for several reasons, but after some running-in at Tyseley (*top left*) No 45596 ventured out onto the main line for the first time (*abov and top centre*). No 45596 then ran with the BLS Support Coach to Stratford-upon-Avon on 15 January 2019 (*above and top right*). All JH

WASHWOOD HEATH, KEIGHLEY and INGROW Seen here at Washwood Heath (*above*), *Bahamas* made a successful loaded test trip from Tyseley to Leicester and back on 31 January 2019. During the test it ran at high speed for parts of the journey, which was a necessary official element of the testing regime. Engine and Support Coach then returned to Keighley (*top right*) and Ingrow (*bottom right*) on 5 February 2019. *John Barrance (top left), JH*

KEIGHLEY and SETTLE *Bahamas* hauled its first rail tour since 1994 on 9 February 2019, running from the KWVR to Carlisle and back, a day of very high winds that caused a 'tree on the line' to delay the train. The pictures show the train about to leave Keighley (*left*) and stopped just outside Keighley (*bottom left*), following permission for the train to proceed at caution to the obstacle so that the Support Crew could assist with its removal. Finally (*bottom right*) No 45596 attacks the S&C at Sheriff Brow, north of Settle. This was the first time a green 'Jubilee' had traversed the S&C since *Bahamas'* last S&C trip on 20 August 1994. Despite the poor weather crowds were out in force! *Terry Neil (2), Maurice Burns*

HORTON-IN-RIBBLESDALE No 45596's first train heads north approaching Horton-in-Ribblesdale on 9 February 2019. *Les Nixon*

LANGWATHBY *Bahamas* is seen heading south in the evening sun at Langwathby on the same day. *John Cooper-Smith*

Second Main-Line Trip, 16 February 2019

STAINFORTH No 45596 heads north with the repeat 'Bahamas Renaissance' tour near Stainforth on 16 February 2019. *Karl Heath*

NEWBIGGIN The return 'Bahamas Renaissance' tour is seen on rising grades near Newbiggin on the same day. *Ian Dixon*

Above right: **OXENHOPE** The Support Crew for the 16 February 2019 train were, from left to right, Graham Allen, Tom Mainprize, Rob Mulvey, Mike Stevens, Steve Peach, Dave Simpson and Gary Davison.

CARLISLE Without a Support Crew it would not be possible to run a steam-hauled rail tour. The BLS team are all volunteers, with some members still employed, which makes rostering difficult at times. The key tasks are illustrated here during the servicing break at Carlisle during No 45596's first trip on 9 February 2019. In addition to checking to see that the engine is mechanically fit, the crew must ensure that the tender tank is full of water and coal, oil round and ensure that the lubrication systems are working effectively, and also to pull – or push – the coal forward. The work is more complicated should it need to be done in the vicinity of electrified lines; safety is of paramount importance at all times. There are strict guidelines as to who can travel in the Support Coach and all members of the 'on train' support team must have passed a Personal Track Safety (PTS) course. While the Driver is in overall control of the train, the BLS has to provide a Responsible Officer (RO) to liaise with the Driver and also control the work of the Support Crew. *All JH*

INGROW *Bahamas* was formally commissioned and returned to traffic on 29 March 2019 by Sir Peter Hendy, Network Rail's Chairman. The event also marked the end of the National Lottery Heritage Fund Project on 31 March, and the opening of the Learning Coach. There was a carnival atmosphere at Ingrow when Sir Peter (*top right and above*) 'commissioned' No 45596, and John Williams from 'The Fund' (*centre left*) accompanied by Keith Whitmore, BLS Chairman, complimented all concerned on the completion of a very successful project. The 'Bahamas Renaissance' headboards, manufactured by Procast Ltd and carried on the engine's first two main-line tours, were sponsored by *The Railway Magazine*, *Steam Railway* magazine and the National Lottery Heritage Fund.

On 29 March the Mortons Media team are seen with one of the headboards in the company of Stephen and James Cliff of Procast Ltd (*far left*). Ian Fisher, CEO of Mortons Media, is seen (*left*) opening the Learning Coach, in the company of Cllr Zafar Ali, Lord Mayor of Bradford. The coach formed the educational element of the project to overhaul *Bahamas*. JH (4), Maurice Burns (2)

KWVR After the ceremonies at Ingrow, *Bahamas* made a spirited run along the KWVR to Oxenhope before returning to Ingrow via Keighley. The train, with the railway's Pullman coaches in the consist, is seen approaching Oxenhope (*top left*) and Oakworth (*top right*). Also seen are John Williams and Kathryn Frankish from the National Lottery Heritage Fund in Leeds (*inset bottom left*), and BLS President Simon Bryant with Peter Robinson from Robinsons Brewery in Stockport (*inset bottom right*). Both Peter and his company were keen supporters of the project to save *Bahamas* in the early days. *Mike Heath, John Cooper-Smith, JH (2)*

How to support No 45596 Bahamas

Want a 'Bahamas Experience'?

If you want to see, hear or travel behind No 45596 *Bahamas* a good starting point would be to visit the BLS website: **(www.bahamas45596.co.uk)**

TYSELEY No 45596 sets off from Tyseley for its Yorkshire home on 5 February 2019. *JH*

Before you leave - ways to help

No 45596 *BAHAMAS* is one of now only a handful of volunteer-owned and operated main-line steam locomotives in the UK. It is supported by the Bahamas Locomotive Society (Charity No 259626), which, despite the help received from the National Heritage Lottery Fund, needs continued support to ensure that it is able to maintain and operate No 45596 properly, and that the commitment to let people see and hear the engine can be fulfilled for as long as possible.

There are various ways to support our work and keep in contact with *Bahamas*. These include:

• **Donate by text** using 'Just Giving'. Text 70070 and enter JUBE35 £5 or JUBE35 £10 (to donate £5 or £10).

• Make a donation to **'Steam's Last Blast Appeal'** either as a one-off donation or by making regular monthly payments as a 'Friend of 45596'. Please see website for details.

• **By joining the Society.** We value the support of 'armchair supporters' as much as those who are able to give some of their time to volunteer in one way or another. Please see website for details.

• By purchasing *Bahamas* **related merchandise.** Available from Ingrow or via the website and on selected *Bahamas*-hauled trains

• By making a **Legacy.**

As the BLS is a Registered Charity, if you are an eligible UK taxpayer you can Gift Aid any donation or Membership Fee, which will increase its value by 25% without incurring any additional cost to yourself.

Details of the ways in which you can help the work of the Society and thus help maintain No 45596 can be found on the BLS website **(www.bahamas45596.co.uk),** by phoning 01535 690 739, or by visiting our Headquarters at Ingrow (BD21 5AX). You can also email: info@ingrowloco.com